Special Occasions

BIRTHDAYS & ANNIVERSARIES

Your Complete List of Dates to Remember

MAGNANIMITY
HOUSE PUBLISHING

Whatever you do or dream you can do —
begin it.
Boldness has genius and power
and magic in it.

—Johann Wolfwang von Goethe

January

January

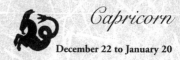

Capricorn
December 22 to January 20

1

Jerome David Salinger 1919: American novelist and short-story writer

2

Samuel Diamond 1931: American Accountant

3

Mel Gibson 1956: Born in Peekskill, NY, Actor

4

Maureen Reagan 1941: American Politician (daughter of 40th US President)

5

Jeane Dixon 1918: American clairvoyant, astrologer, columnist and writer

6

Loretta Young 1912: American actress

7

Nicholas Cage 1964: Born in Long Beach, CA, Actor

January

8

Elvis Presley 1935: American singer and actor

9

Richard Nixon 1913: American Politician, 37th US President

10

Donald Fagen 1948: Born in Passaic, NJ, Singer and keyboardist

11

William James 1842: American teacher, philosopher and writer

12

Howard Stern 1954: Born in New York, NY, Radio DJ

13

Penelope Ann Miller 1964: Born in Santa Monica, CA, Actress

14

Andy Rooney 1919: American columnist, writer and broadcast journalist

15

Moliere 1622: French playwright

16

Kate Moss 1974: Born in London, England, Supermodel

17

Jim Carrey 1962: Born in Jackson Point, Canada, Actor

18

Kevin Costner 1955: Born in Lynwood, CA, Actor, director, producer

19

Dolly Pardon 1946: American singer, songwriter, musician and actress

20

George Burns 1896: American actor and comedian

21

Geena Davis 1957: Born in Wareham, MA, Actress

January

22

John Russell 1919: English art historian, columnist and critic

23

Jeanne Moreau 1928: French Actress

24

Vicki Baum 1896: American novelist and playwright

25

Virginia Wolf 1882: English novelist and essayist

26

Wayne Gretzky 1961: Born in Bradford, Canada, Hockey player

27

Bridget Fonda 1964: Born in Los Angeles, CA, Actress

28

Arthur Rubenstein 1887: American pianist

January

29

Oprah Winfrey 1954: Born in Kosciusko, MS, Talk-show host

30

Brett Butler 1958: Born in Montgomery, AL, Actress

31

Suzanne Pleshette 1937: American actress

Make no little plans.
They have no magic to stir man's blood.
Make big plans; aim high in hope and work.

—D.H. Burnham

February

February

1

Lisa Marie Presley-Jackson 1968: Born in Memphis, TN, Daughter of Elvis and Priscilla Presley

2

Christie Brinkley 1954: Born in Malibu, CA, Supermodel

3

Clint Black 1962: Born in Long Beach, NJ, Singer, songwriter

4

Barbara Hershey 1948: Born in Hollywood, CA, Actress

5

Red Buttons (Aaron Chwatt) 1919: Born in New York, NY, Performer

6

Natalie Cole 1949: Born in Los Angeles, CA, (Daughter of Nat King Cole), Singer

7

Garth Brooks 1962: Born in Tulsa, OK, Singer, songwriter

February

8

Ted Koppel 1940: Born in Lancashire, England, Broadcast journalist

9

Mia Farrow 1945: Born in Los Angeles, CA, Actress

10

Mimi Sheraton 1926: American food writer and critic

11

Leslie Nielsen 1926: Born in Regina, Canada, Actor, writer

12

Arsenio Hall 1959: Born in Cleveland, OH, Talk-show host

13

Stockard Channing 1944: Born in New York, NY, Actress

14

Jack Benny 1894: American actor and comedian

February

15

Jane Seymour 1951: Born in Hilling, Middlesex, England, Actress

16

Edgar Bergen 1903: American entertainer and ventriloquist

17

Michael Jordan 1963: Born in Brooklyn, NY, Basketball player and retired baseball player

18

John Travolta 1954: American Actor

19

Lee Marvin 1924: Actor

20

Charles Barkley 1963: Born in Leeds, AL, Basketball player

21

Tyne Daly 1946: Born in Madison, WI, Actress

February

22

Drew Barrymore 1975: Born in Los Angeles, CA, Actress

23

Leslie Halliwell 1929: English film consultant, writer and critic

24

George Moore 1852: Irish novelist, poet, playwright and journalist

25

Jim Backus 1913: Actor

26

Michael Bolton 1953: Born in New Haven, CT, Singer, songwriter

27

Elizabeth Taylor 1932: Born in London, England, Actress

28/29

Michell de Montaigne 1533: French essayist and philosopher

You see things; and you say "Why?"
But I dream things that never were;
and I say "Why not?"

—George Bernard Shaw

March

March

1

Ron Howard 1954: Actor and director

2

John Irving 1942: Born in Exeter, NH, Author

3

Jean Harlow 1911: Actress

4

Robert Orben 1927: Speech writer and comedy writer

5

Andy Gibb 1958: English musician

6

Tom Arnold 1959: Born in Ottumwa, IA, Actor

7
Alessandro Manzoni 1785: Italian poet and novelist

March

8

Gene Fowler 1890: Novelist, journalist, playwright and biographer

9

Mickey Spillane 1918: Novelist

10

Sharon Stone 1958: Born in Meadville, PA, Actress

11

Dana Delany 1956: Born in New York, NY, Actress

12

Andrew Young 1932: Clergyman, civil rights leader, politician and diplomat

13

Paul Fix 1902: Actor, director, producer and screenwriter

14

Michael Caine 1933: Born in London, England, Actor

15

Norm Van Brocklin 1926: Football player and coach

16

Jerry Lewis 1926: Actor, comedian, producer and director

17

Rob Lowe 1964: Born in Charlottesville, VA, Actor

18

John Updike 1932: Novelist, poet and short-story writer

19

Glenn Close 1947: Born in Greenwich, CT, Actress

20

Holly Hunter 1958: Born in Conyers, GA, Actress

21

Matthew Broderick 1962: Born in New York, NY, Actor

March

22

William Shatner 1931: Born in Montreal, Canada, Actor, author, producer and director

23

Marty Allen 1922: Comedian

24

Dwight MacDonald 1906: Journalist, editor, writer and critic

25

Aretha Franklin 1942: Born in Memphis, TN, Singer

26

Steven Tyler 1948: Born in Boston, MA, Played in rock band

27

Mariah Carey 1970: Born in New York, NY, Singer

28

Reba Mcentire 1955: Born in McAlester, OK, Singer and songwriter

March

29

Jennifer Capriati 1976: Born in Long Island, NY, Tennis player

30

Warren Beatty 1937: Born in Richmond, VA, Actor, producer, director and screenwriter

31

Henry Morgan 1915: Actor and comedian

The world is divided into people who do things
and people who get credit.
Try, if you can, to belong to the first class.
There's far less competition.

—Dwight Morrow

April

April

1

Agnes Repplier 1855: American essayist

2

Dana Carvey 1955: Born in Missoula, MT, Actor

3

Alec Baldwin 1958: Born in Massapequa, NY, Actor

4

Robert Downey 1965: Born in New York, NY, Actor

5

Bette Davis 1908: Actress

6

Sylvester Stallone 1946: Born in Hell's Kitchen, NY, Actor, writer and director

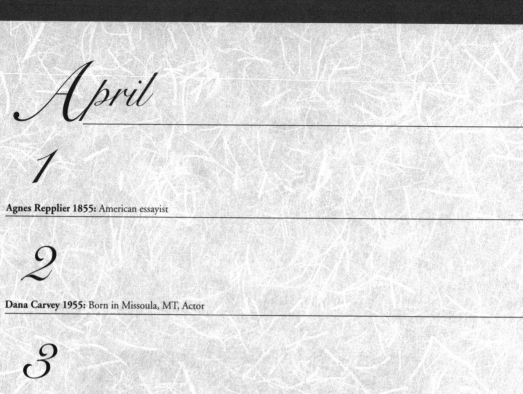

7

Francis Ford Coppola 1939: Born in Detroit, MI, Director and writer

April

8

Sonja Henie 1912: Norwegian skater and actress

9

Dennis Quaid 1954: Born in Houston, TX, Actor

10

Steven Seagal 1951: Born in Lansing, MI, Actor and producer

11

Dean Acheson 1893: Lawyer, statesman and US Secretary of State

12

David Cassidy 1950: Born in New York, NY, Actor

13

Peabo Bryson 1951: Born in Greenville, SC, Singer

14

Loretta Lynn 1935: Born in Butcher Hollow, KY, Singer and songwriter

April

15

Emma Thompson 1959: Born in London, England, Actress

16

Ellen Barkin 1954: Born in Bronx, NY, Actress

17

Debra Winger 1955: Born in Cleveland, OH, Actress

18

Conan O'Brien 1963: Born in Brookline, MA, Talk-show host and writer

19

Jayne Mansfield 1932: Actress

20

Luther Vandross 1951: Born in New York, NY, Singer and songwriter

21

Charles Grodin 1935: Born in Pittsburgh, PA, Actor and writer

April

22

Jack Nicholson 1937: Born in Neptune, NJ, Actor, director, producer and screenwriter

23

William Shakespeare 1564: Poet and playwright

24

Shirley Maclaine 1934: Born in Richmond, VA, Actress

25

Al Pacino 1939: Born in New York, NY, Actor

26

Carol Burnett 1933: Comedian, actress and singer

27

Anouk Aimee 1934: Born in Paris, France, Actor

28

Jay Leno 1950: Born in Rochelle, NY, Talk-show host and comedian

April

29

Andre Agassi 1970: Born in Las Vegas, NV, Tennis player

30

Willie Nelson 1933: Born in Abbott, TX, Singer, Songwriter, quitarist and actor

No person was ever honoured
for what he received.
Honor has been the reward
for what he gave.

—Calvin Coolidge

May

May

1
Glen Ford 1916: Actor

2
Jon Bon Jovi 1962: Born in Sayreville, NJ, Singer and songwriter

3
Wyonna Judd 1964: Born in Ashland, KY, Singer

4
Nickolas Ashford 1942: Born in Fairfield, SC, Singer

5
Tyrone Power 1914: Actor

6
Orson Welles 1915: Actor, producer, director and writer

7
Johnny Unitas 1933: Football player and restaurateur

May

8

Melissa Gilbert 1964: Born in Los Angeles, CA, Actress

9

Candice Bergen 1946: Born in Beverly Hills, CA, Actress and photojournalist

10

Bono (Paul Hewson) 1960: Born in Dublin, Ireland, Singer and songwriter

11

Phil Silvers 1912: Comedian and actor

12

Tom Snyder 1936: Born in Milwaukee, WI, Talk-show host

13

Arthur Sullivan 1842: English composer and conductor

14

David Byrne 1952: Born in Dumbarton, Scotland, Singer, songwriter and director

May

15

Joseph Cotten 1905: Actor

16

Pierce Brosnan 1952: Born in Novan, Meath County, Ireland, Actor

17

Erik Satie 1866: French composer

18

Herbert Prochnow 1897: Speech writer, editor, humorist and economist

19

Nora Ephron 1941: Journalist, writer and editor

20

Cher 1946: Born in El Centro, CA, Actress and singer

21

Harold Robbins 1916: Novelist

May

22

Robert Byrne 1930: Writer

23

Douglas Fairbanks 1883: Actor and producer

24

Rosanne Cash 1955: Born in Memphis, TN, Singer and songwriter

25

Bennett Cerf 1898: Publisher, editor, columnist and humorist

26

John Wayne 1907: Actor

27

Henry Kissinger 1923: Political scientist and US Secretary of State

28

Tom Scott 1912: Composer, singer and musician

May

29

Annette Bening 1958: Born in Topeka, KS, Actress

30

Keir Dullea 1936: Born in Cleveland, OH, Actor

31

Clint Eastwood 1930: Born in San Fransico, CA, Actor, producer and director

*Snowflakes are one of nature's
most fragile things,
but just look what they can do
when they stick together.*

—Vesta M. Kelly

June

June

1
Marilyn Monroe 1926: Actress

2
Nubar Gulbenkian 1896: Iranian oil man and financier

3
Tony Curtis 1925: Actor

4
Roger Ball 1944: Born in Dundee, Scotland, Alto and baritone saxophonist

5
John Maynard Keynes 1927: English economist, journalist and financier

6
Maria Montez 1860: Actress

7
Prince 1958, Born in Minneapolis, MN, Singer, songwriter and actor

June

8

Joan Rivers 1937: Born in Brooklyn, NY, Talk-show host

9

Michael J. Fox 1961: Born in Edmonton, Canada, Actor

10

Prince Philip 1921: English royalty (husband of Queen Elizabeth II)

11

Vince Lombardi 1913: Football coach

12

Timothy Busfield 1957: Born in Lansing, MI, Actor

13

Tim Allen 1953, Born in Denver, CO, Actor and comedian

14

Rod Argent 1945: Born in St. Albans, England, Keyboardist

June

15

Herman Smith-Johannsen 1875: Canadian skier

16

Joan van Ark 1943: Born in New York, NY, Actress

17

Barry Manilow 1946: Born in Brooklyn, NY, Singer and songwriter

18

Roger Ebert 1942: Born in Urbana, IL, Film critic and writer

19

Kathleen Turner 1954: Born in Springfield, MO, Actress

20

John Goodman 1952: Born in Afton, MO, Actor

21

Juliette Lewis 1973: Born in San Fernando Valley, CA, Actress

June

22

Meryl Streep 1949: Born in Summit, NJ, Actress

23

Alfred Kinsey 1894: Zoologist

24

Phil Harris 1906: Actor and band leader

25

Sidney Lumet 1924: Director

26

Babe Zaharias 1914: Athlete

27

Ross Perot 1930: Born in Texarkana, TX, Businessman

28

Kathy Bates 1948: Born in Memphis, TN, Actress

June

29

Joan Davis 1907: Actress and comedian

30

Florence Ballard 1943: Born in Detroit, MI, Singer

*When you cannot make up your mind
which of two evenly balanced
courses of action you should take —
choose the bolder one.*

—W.J. Slim

July

July

1

Dan Aykroyd 1952: Born in Ottawa, Canada, Actor and writer

2

Robert Sarnoff 1918: Broadcasting executive

3

Tom Cruise 1962: Born in Syracuse, NY, Actor

4

Neil Simon 1927: Born in Bronx, NY, Singer and songwriter

5

Jean Cocteau 1889: Poet, novelist, painter, actor, director and filmmaker

6

Nancy Reagan 1923: Actress and wife of 40th US President

7

Robert Heinlein 1907: Science fiction writer

July

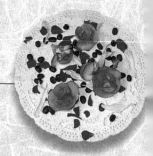

8

Kevin Bacon 1958: Born in Philadelphia, PA, Actor

9

Tom Hanks 1956: Born in Concord, CA, Actor

10

Jean Kerr 1923: American playwright

11

Giorgio Armani 1934: Born in Piacenza, Italy, Fashion designer

12

Bill Cosby 1937: Born in Philadelphia, PA, Actor, comedian, producer and author

13

Harrison Ford 1942: Born in Chicago, IL, Actor and director

14

Gerald Ford 1913: Politician and 38th US President

July

15

Willie Upton 1960: Born in Los Angeles, CA, Actor

16

Ginger Rogers 1911: Dancer and actress

17

David Hasselhoff 1952: Born in Baltimore, MD, Actor

18

Nelson Mandela 1918: Born in Umtata, South Aftica, President, South Africa

19

Herbert Marcuse 1898, Political philosopher, teacher and writer

20

Natalie Wood 1938: Actress

21

Rob Morrow 1962: Born in New Rochelle, NY, Actor

22

Don Henley 1947: Born in Linden, TX, Singer, songwriter, drummer and guitarist

23

Woody Harrelson 1961: Born in Midland, TX, Actor

24

Alexandre Dumas 1802: French novelist and playwright

25

Eric Hoffer 1902: Longshoreman, writer and philosopher

26

Mick Jagger 1943: Born in Dartford, England, Singer and songwriter

27

Leo Durocher 1906: Baseball player and manager

28

Melvin Belli 1907: Lawyer and writer

July

29

Peter Jennings 1938: Born in Toronto, Canada, TV Journalist

30

Arnold Schwarzenegger 1947: Born in Graz, Austria, Actor, director and bodybuilder

31

Wesley Snipes 1963: Born in Orlando, FL, Actor

What counts is not the number of hours you put in, but how much you put in the hours.

—Unknown

August

August

1

Robert James Waller 1939: Born in Rockford, Iowa, Auther and professor of business management

2

James Baldwin 1924: Novelist, essayist and playwright

3

Tony Bennett 1926: Born in Astoria, NY, Singer

4

Oscar Ameringer 1870: Editor, publisher, writer, musician, painter and Socialist party leader

5

Hugh Johnson 1882: Army officer, journalist and government administrator

6

Andy Warhol 1927: Painter, sculptor, magazine publisher, filmmaker and writer

7

Mata Hari 1876: Dutch dancer, courtesan and spy

August

8

Keith Carradine 1951: Born in San Mateo, CA, Actor

9

Melanie Griffith 1957: Born in New York, NY, Actress

10

Louis Sobol 1896: Journalist

11

Hulk Hogan 1953: Wrestler and actor

12

George Hamilton 1939: Actor

13

Alfred Hitchcock 1899: English director

14

Halle Berry 1968: Born in Cleveland, OH, Actress

August

15

Julia Child 1912: Cookbook writer and television personality

16

Angela Bassett 1958: Born in New York, NY, Actress

17

Robert De Niro 1943: Born in New York, NY, Actor

18

Robert Redford 1937: Born in Santa Monica, CA, Actor, director and producer

19

Malcolm Forbes 1919: Publisher, editor and sportsman

20

Connie Chung 1946: Born in Washington, DC, TV Journalist

21

Peter Anderson 1940: Lawyer

22

Dorothy Parker 1893: Poet, short-story writer and critic

23

Gene Kelly 1912: Dancer, director and actor

24

Claudia Schiffer 1971: Born in Germany, Supermodel

25

Sean Connery 1930: Born in Edinburgh, Scotland, Actor

26

Macaulay Culkin 1980: Born in New York, NY, Actor

27

Frank Leahy 1908: Football coach

28

Charles Wright Mills 1916: Teacher and sociologist

August

29

Michael Jackson 1958: Born in Gary, IN, Singer, song writer and actor

30

Elizabeth Ashley 1939: Born in Ocala, FL, Actor

31

Richard Gere 1948: Born in Philadelphia, PA, Actor

*If you really know what you want out of life,
it's amazing how opportunities
will come to enable you to carry them out.*

—John M. Goddard

September

September

1
Lily Tomlin 1939: Comedian and actress

2
Keanu Reeves 1964: Born in Beirut, Lebanon, Actor

3
Charlie Sheen 1965: Born in New York, NY, Actor

4
Paul Harvey 1918: Columnist and broadcast journalist

5
John Cage 1912: Composer, teacher, writer and poet

6

Billy Rose 1899: Songwriter and theatrical producer.

7
Grandma Moses 1860: Folk painter

September

8

Denise Darcel 1925: Actress and singer

9

Sylvia Miles 1932: Actress and comedian

10

Karl Lagerfeld 1938: Born in Hamburg, Germany, Fashion designer

11

Harry Connick Jr. 1967: Born in New Orleans, LA, Singer

12

Linda Gray 1940: Born in Santa Monica, CA, Actress

13

Sherwood Anderson 1876: Novelist, poet and short-story writer

14

Pete Agnew 1946: Born in Scotland, Singer

September

15

Tommy Lee Jones 1946: Born in San Saba, TX, Actor

16

David Copperfield 1956: Born in Metuchen, NJ, Magician

17

Anne Bancroft 1931: Born in Bronx, NY, Actress

18

Joseph Story 1779: Lawyer, teacher and US Supreme Court Justice

19

Jeremy Irons 1948: Born in Cowes, Isle of Wight, England, Actor

20

Sophia Loren 1934: Actress

21

Stephen King 1947: Born in Portland, ME, Author

September

Libra

September 24 to October 23

22

Shari Belafonte 1954: Born in New York, NY, Actress

23

Bruce Springsteen 1949: Born in Freehold, NY, Rock singer

24

Phil Hartman 1948: Born in Ontario, Canada, Actor and writer

25

Michael Douglas 1944: Born in New Brunswick, NJ, Actor, producer and director

26

George Raft 1895: Actor

27

Meat Loaf (Marvin Lee Aday) 1947: Born in Dallas, TX, Singer

28

Brigitte Bardot 1934: Actress

September

29

Richard Harkness 1907: Journalist and broadcaster

30

Truman Capote 1924: Novelist, short-story writer and playwright

Remember that you are needed.
There is at least one important work to be done
that will not be done unless you do it.

—Charles Allen

October

October

1

Julie Andrews 1935: Actress and singer

2

Donna Karan 1948: Born in Forest Hills, NY, Fashion designer

3

Thomas Wolfe 1900: Novelist

4

Alvin Toffler 1928: Journalist, teacher and writer

5

Josie Bissett 1969: Born in Seattle, WA, Actress

6

Carole Lombard 1908: Actress

7

Desmond Tutu 1931: South African teacher, clergyman and political activist

October

8

Chevy Chase 1943: Born in New York, NY, Actor

9

Scott Bakula 1955: Born in St. Louis, MO, Actor

10

Jessica Harper 1949: Born in Chicago, IL, Actress

11

Luke Perry 1966: Born in Frederickton, OH, Actor

12

Luciano Pavarotti 1935: Born in Modena, Italy, Opera singer

13

Paul Simon 1941: Born in Newark, NJ, Singer and songwriter

14

Ralph Lauren 1939: Born in Bronx, NY, Fashion designer

October

15

Penny Marshall 1942: Born in New York, NY, Actress and director

16

Angela Lansbury 1925: Born in London, England, Actress

17

Barnaby Keeney 1914: Historian and educator

18

Martina Navratilova 1956: Born in Prague, Czechoslovakia, Tennis player

19

Lewis Mumford 1895: Historian, city planner, teacher and writer

20

Adolph Deutsch 1897: Composer and conductor

21

Carrie Fisher 1956: Born in Burbank, CA, Actress, novelist and screenwriter

October

22

Jeff Goldblum 1952: Born in Pittsburgh, PA, Actor

23

Johnny Carson 1925: Born in Corning, IA, Talk-show host

24

Abraham F. Murray 1939: Born in Pittsburgh, PA, Actor

25

Anne Tyler 1941: Novelist

26

Hillary Rodham Clinton 1947: Born in Park Ridge, IL, First Lady

27

Jack Carson 1910: Canadian actor and comedian

28

Michael Crichton 1942: Born in Chicago, IL, Writer and director

October

29

Richard Dreyfuss 1947: Born in Brooklyn, NY, Actor

30

Ruth Gordon 1896: Actress and screenwriter

31

Lee Grant 1929: Actress

God grant us the serenity
to accept what cannot be changed;
give us the courage to change
what should be changed;
give us the wisdom
to distinguish one from another.

—Reinhold Niebuhr

November

November

1

Lyle Lovett 1957: Born in Klein, TX, Singer and songwriter

2

Burt Lancaster 1913: Actor

3

Roseanne Bar 1952: Born in Salt Lake City, UT, Actress

4

Yanni Kalamata 1954: Born in Greece

5

Bryan Adams 1959: Born in Kingston, Canada, Singer, songwriter and guitarist

6

Sally Field 1946: Born in Pasadena, CA, Actress

7

Joan Sutherland 1926: Australian opera singer

November

8

Katharine Hepburn 1907: Born in Hartford, CT, Actress

9

Spiro Agnew 1918: Lawyer, politician and 39th US Vice President

10

Sinbad (David Adkins) 1956: Born in Benton Harbor, MI, Actor and comedian

11

Demi Moore 1962: Born in Roswell, NM, Actress

12

Elizabeth Cady Stanton 1815: American leader of women's suffrage movement

13

Whoopi Goldberg 1949: Born in New York, NY, Actress

14

Prince Charles 1948: English royalty (son of Queen Elizabeth II)

November

15

Franklin Adams 1881: Journalist

16

George Kaufman 1889: Playwright and critic

17

Danny Devito 1944: Born in Neptune, NJ, Actor, director and producer

18

Dorothy Dix 1870: Advice columnist

19

Jodie Foster 1962: Born in Los Angeles, CA, Actress and director

20

Robert Kennedy 1925: Lawyer, politician and US Attorney General

21

Goldie Hawn 1945: Born in Takoma Park, MD, Actress

22

Jamie Lee Curtis 1958: Born in Los Angeles, CA, Actress

23

"Willie the Lion" Smith 1897: Jazz Pianist

24

William F. Buckley Jr. 1925: Editor, columnist, television interviewer and writer

25

Amy Grant 1960: Born in Augusta, GA, Singer

26

Charles Schulz 1922: Cartoonist

27

James Agee 1909: Novelist, poet and film critic

28

Paul Shaffer 1949: Born in Thunder Bay, Ontario, Canada, Musician and bandleader

November

29

George Gilder 1939: Economist and writer

30

Bo Jackson 1962: Born in Bessemer, AL, Football player and baseball player

Do what is right,
do it because it's right,
then do it right.

-Unknown

December

December

1

Woody Allen 1935: Born in Brooklyn, NY, Actor, director and writer

2

Russell Lynes 1910: Editor and writer

3

Ozzy Osbourne 1948: Born in Aston, England, Singer

4

Jeff Bridges 1949: Born in Los Angeles, CA, Actor

5

Walt Disney 1901: Producer and animation pioneer

6

Steven Wright 1955: Actor and comedian

7

Robert (Bo) Belinsky 1936: Baseball player

December

8

Kim Basinger 1953: Born in Athens, GA, Actress

9

Beau Bridges 1941: Born in Los Angeles, CA

10

Emily Dickinson 1830: Poet

11

Fiorella La Guardia 1882: Lawyer and politician

12

Frank Sinatra 1915: Born in Hoboken, NJ, Singer and actor

13

George Shultz 1920: Economist and US Secretary of State

14

Leon Botsteen 1946: Educator, historian and musician

December

15

Don Johnson 1949: Born in Flat Creek, MO, Actor

16

Steven Bochco 1943: Born in New York, NY, Producer and screenwriter

17

William Safire 1929: Columnist and writer

18

Brad Pitt 1963: Born in Shawnee, OK, Actor

19

Ralph Richardson 1902: English actor

20

Hortense Calisher 1911: Novelist

21

Phil Donahue 1935: Born in Cleveland, OH, Talk-show host

December

22

Diane Sawyer 1945: Born in Glasgow, KY, Broadcast journalist

23

Susan Lucci 1948: Born in Scarsdale, NY, Actress

24

Ava Gardner 1922: Actress

25

Jimmy Buffett 1946: Born in Pascagoula, MS, Singer and songwriter

26

Alan King 1927: Comedian and producer

27

Oscar Levant 1906: Pianist, composer, actor and writer

28

Sam Levenson 1856: Comedian and writer

December

29

Ted Danson 1947: Born in San Diego, CA, Actor

30

Stephen Leacock 1869: Canadian educator, economist, writer and humorist

31

Anthony Hopkins 1937: Born in Port Talbot, South Wales, Actor

Chinese Astrology

Mouse

Honest, ambitious, charming. Quick to anger. Penny-pinching towards others.
Gossipy. Persevering. A poor leader, a big spender. Energetic.

YOUR LIFE LINE

First Phase:	Fair and warm.
Second Phase:	Storms.
Third Phase:	Clearing skies.
You should marry:	Dragon, monkey, ox.
You could marry:	Mouse, tiger, snake, dog, pig.
You should not marry:	Horse.

1900
1912
1924
1936
1948
1960
1972
1984
1996

Ox

The quiet type. Patient, easy-going with a gift for inspiring confidence.
Often narrow-minded and stubborn. A terror when angered. Dexterous and strong.

YOUR LIFE LINE

First Phase:	Generally happy.
Second Phase:	Family, marital difficulties.
Third Phase:	Smoother.
You should marry:	Snake, mouse, rooster.
You could marry:	Ox, dragon, rabbit, monkey, pig.
You should not marry:	Horse, dog, sheep.

1901
1913
1925
1937
1949
1961
1973
1985
1997

Tiger

True blue with friends, wary of strangers. Fighting spirit. A dilly-dallier on decisions.
Sensitive, deep thinking, stubbornly courageous. Troublesome temper.

YOUR LIFE LINE

First Phase:	Easy.
Second Phase:	Handle problems carefully.
Third Phase:	With care no troubles.
You should marry:	Horse, dragon, dog.
You could marry:	Mouse, ox, rabbit, tiger, sheep, pig, rooster.
You should not marry:	Snake, monkey.

1902
1914
1926
1938
1950
1962
1974
1986
1998

Rabbit

Affectionate in reserved way. Virtuous, placid, quietly talented. Born gambler.
Not a go-getter. Low on curiosity. Melancholic. Easy to befriend.

YOUR LIFE LINE

First Phase:	Placid.
Second Phase:	Placid.
Third Phase:	Placid.
You should marry:	Sheep, dog, pig.
You could marry:	Dragon.
You should not marry:	Mouse, rooster.

1903
1915
1927
1939
1951
1963
1975
1987
1999

Chinese Astrology

Dragon

Excitable, short-tempered, stubborn on the outside, honest, sensitive, soft-hearted on the inside. Worrisome, fastidious, verbose, but for all of that, beloved. A leader of men.

YOUR LIFE LINE

First Phase:	Fastidious brings difficulties.
Second Phase:	In and out.
Third Phase:	Peace at last.
You should marry:	Mouse, snake, monkey, rooster.
You could marry:	Tiger, horse, sheep, pig.
You should not marry:	Ox, rabbit, dragon, dog.

1904
1916
1928
1940
1952
1964
1976
1988
2000

Snake

Extremely wise and attractive but also vain and self-centered. Passionate, determined, rather egotistic. A winner, with money. Too much heart. Deep and Quiet.

YOUR LIFE LINE

First Phase:	People problems.
Second Phase:	Confine love to family.
Third Phase:	Handle with care.
You should marry:	Ox, rooster.
You could marry:	Mouse, rabbit, dragon, snake, monkey, tiger, pig.
You should not marry:	Horse, sheep, dog.

1905
1917
1929
1941
1953
1965
1977
1989
2001

Horse

Quick in everything. Handy with money. Flattery gets you everywhere. Showy in dress. Always a winner. Cheerful, popular, loquacious. Hot blooded, stubborn.

YOUR LIFE LINE

First Phase:	Much trouble.
Second Phase:	More of same.
Third Phase:	A good life at last.
You should marry:	Tiger, dog, sheep.
You could marry:	Dragon, snake, monkey, rooster, pig.
You should not marry:	Ox, rabbit, horse, mouse.

1906
1918
1930
1942
1954
1966
1978
1990
2002

Sheep

A poor salesman. Never a world leader. Passionate in everything. Best at the arts. Talents will always bring money. Easily stimulated to pity. Charitable. Elegant.

YOUR LIFE LINE

First Phase:	No clouds visible.
Second Phase:	Love, emotional problems.
Third Phase:	Extra good fortune.
You should marry:	Rabbit, pig, horse.
You could marry:	Tiger, dragon, snake, sheep, monkey, rooster.
You should not marry:	Mouse, ox, dog.

1907
1919
1931
1943
1955
1967
1979
1991
2003

Chinese Astrology

Monkey

A big thinker, big doer. A good politician. Cleaver, inventive, flexible.
Have little stick-to-it-iveness. Thirsty for knowledge. Talented, self-willed. Passionate.

YOUR LIFE LINE

First Phase:	Possible fame awaits.
Second Phase:	Distracted and confused.
Third Phase:	Success indicated if you stay on course.
You should marry:	Dragon, mouse.
You could marry:	Rabbit, sheep, dog.
You should not marry:	Snake, pig, tiger.

1908
1920
1932
1944
1956
1968
1980
1992
2004

Rooster

A loner. Deep thinking and short-sighted. Tactless. Big dreams, little acts.
Ambitious and brave. Idealistic. Someone disliked, but never a bore.

YOUR LIFE LINE

First Phase:	Ambition could prevail.
Second Phase:	Outspokenness could harm friendships.
Third Phase:	Fortune resembles waves.
You should marry:	Ox, Snake, dragon.
You could marry:	Tiger, horse, sheep, monkey, pig.
You should not marry:	Mouse, dog, rabbit, rooster.

1909
1921
1933
1945
1957
1969
1981
1993
2005

Dog

Pillar of the community, devoted and honest. As stubborn as they come.
Oblivious of money, but never in want. Fault-finder. Poor small talk. Leader of men.

YOUR LIFE LINE

First Phase:	Earmarked for success.
Second Phase:	Promising talents.
Third Phase:	Could become famous.
You should marry:	Horse, tiger, rabbit.
You could marry:	Mouse, snake, dog, pig.
You should not marry:	Ox, dragon, sheep, rooster.

1910
1922
1934
1946
1958
1970
1982
1994
2006

Pig

Dedicated and courageous, with remarkable integrity. Shy, single-minded, short-tempered.
Affectionate and kind to loved ones. Impulsive and honest, so avoid lawsuits.

YOUR LIFE LINE

First Phase:	Difficulties.
Second Phase:	More difficulties.
Third Phase:	Success through personal efforts.
You should marry:	Mouse, ox, tiger, dragon, horse.
You could marry:	Dog, rooster.
You should not marry:	Mouse, pig, snake.

1911
1923
1935
1947
1959
1971
1983
1995
2007

Months of the Year

January

- first month of the year
- 31 days
- named for the Roman god Janus
- means gates and doors symbolizes openings or beginnings and good endings
  Birthstone: Garnet
  Flower: Carnation, snowdrop
  Symbolizes: Constancy

April

- fourth month of the year
- 30 days
- derived from the Latin word 'aperire' which means to open
- a reference to spring and opening of the floral buds
  Birthstone: Diamond
  Flower: Sweet pea, daisy
  Symbolizes: Innocence

February

- second month of the year
- 28 days, every four years 29 days (leap year)
- is derived from the Latin word 'Februa' which means purification
  Birthstone: Amethyst
  Flower: Violet, primrose
  Symbolizes: Sincerity

May

- fifth month of the year
- 31 days
- means "prime" as in the prime of life
- month of celebrations, i.e.: May Day, Memorial Day, Mothers' Day
  Birthstone: Emerald
  Flower: Lily of the valley
  Symbolizes: Love and success

March

- third month of the year
- 31 days
- named for Mars the god of spring
- until the Georgian calender was adopted March 25 was considered the first of the year
  Birthstone: Aquamarine, bloodstone
  Flower: Daffodil
  Symbolizes: Courage

June

- sixth month of the year
- 30 days
- derived from the Roman god Juno
- dedicated to youth and old age
- Juno was the protector of women who proceeded over marriages and child birth, i.e.: June bride
  Birthstone: Pearl, alexandrite, moonstone
  Flower: Rose, honey suckle
  Symbolizes: Health and longevity

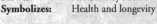

Months of the Year

July

- seventh month of the year
- 31 days
- named for "Julius Caesar" for it was the month he was born

Birthstone:	Ruby
Flower:	Larkspur, water lily
Symbolizes:	Contentment

August

- eighth month of the year
- 31 days
- originally named 'Sextilis'
- name change to honor the Roman Emperor 'Augustus'

Birthstone:	Peridot, sardongy
Flower:	Poppy, gladiola
Symbolizes:	Married, happiness

September

- ninth month of the year
- 30 days
- derived from the Latin word 'Septem' means seven
- originally it was the seventh month of the Roman calendar

Birthstone:	Sapphire
Flower:	Aster, morning glory
Symbolizes:	Clear thinking

October

- tenth month of the year
- 31 days
- derived from the Latin word 'Octo' which means eight originally it was the eighth month of the Roman calendar
- month of harvest
- celebrated with many year end festivals, before winter

Birthstone:	Opal, tourmaline
Flower:	Calendula, cosmos
Symbolizes:	Hope

November

- eleventh month of the year
- 30 days
- derived from the Latin word 'Novembris' means ninth
- it was the ninth month of the Roman calendar

Birthstone:	Topaz
Flower:	Chrysanthemum
Symbolizes:	Fidelity

December

- twelfth month of the year
- 31 days
- festive month, it has taken on the Christian Christmas season and the Jewish holiday Hanukkah
- originally the Roman holiday 'Saturnalia' honoring the god Saturn

Birthstone:	Turquoise, zircon
Flower:	Narcissus, holly
Symbolizes:	Prosperity

Anniversaries

1st	Paper		14th	Ivory
2nd	Cotton		15th	Crystal
3rd	Leather		20th	Porcelain
4th	Silk flowers		25th	Silver
5th	Wood		30th	Pearl
6th	Iron or candy		35th	Coral
7th	Copper or wool		40th	Ruby
8th	Bronze or rubber		45th	Sapphire
9th	Pottery		50th	Gold
10th	Tin		55th	Emerald
11th	Steel		60th	Diamond
12th	Linen		75th	Diamond
13th	Lace			

Wife's Family Tree

Name
_____

Birthplace _____ Date _____

Brothers and Sisters
_____

Father

Name
_____

Birthplace _____ Date _____

Paternal Grandparents

Grandfather
_____

Birthplace _____ Date _____

Grandmother
_____

Birthplace _____ Date _____

Paternal

Grandfather's Father
_____

Birthplace _____ Date _____

Grandfather's Mother
_____

Birthplace _____ Date _____

Grandmother's Father
_____

Birthplace _____ Date _____

Grandmother's Mother
_____

Birthplace _____ Date _____

Mother

Name
_____

Birthplace _____ Date _____

Maternal Grandparents

Grandfather
_____

Birthplace _____ Date _____

Grandmother
_____

Birthplace _____ Date _____

Maternal

Grandfather's Father
_____

Birthplace _____ Date _____

Grandfather's Mother
_____

Birthplace _____ Date _____

Grandmother's Father
_____

Birthplace _____ Date _____

Grandmother's Mother
_____

Birthplace _____ Date _____